TOWARD THE ZEN

OF PERFORMANCE

Music Improvisation Therapy
for the Development of
Self-Confidence in the Performer

Dorita S. Berger
MA, MT-BC

MMB MUSIC, INC.

TOWARD THE ZEN OF PERFORMANCE

Music Improvisation Therapy for the Development
of Self-Confidence in the Performer

Dorita S. Berger, MA, MT-BC

© Copyright 1999 MMB Music, Inc. All rights reserved. International protection secured under Berne, UCC, Buenos Aires, and bilateral copyright treaties. No part of this publication may be reproduced, stored in a retrieval system, or transmitted—in any form or by any means now known or later developed—without prior written permission except in the case of brief quotations embodied in critical articles and reviews.

Cover Design: Lynne Condellone
Printer: Flambeau Litho Corp., Ladysmith, Wisconsin
First Printing: July 1999
Printed in USA
ISBN: 1-58106-010-6

For information and catalogs contact:

MMB Music, Inc.
Contemporary Arts Building
3526 Washington Avenue
Saint Louis, MO 63103-1019 USA

Phone: 314 531-9635, 800 543-3771 (USA/Canada)
Fax: 314 531-8384
E-mail: mmbmusic@mmbmusic.com
Web site: http://www.mmbmusic.com

Every Master who practices an art molded by Zen is like a flash of lightening from the cloud of all-encompassing Truth. This Truth is present in the free movement of his spirit, and he meets it again, in "IT," as his own, original and nameless essence. He meets his essence over and over again as his own being's utmost possibilities, so that the Truth assumes for him—and for others through him—a thousand shapes and forms....

—Eugene Herrigel,
Zen in the Art of Archery

Contents

Acknowledgments

To the performing musicians who risk sharing parts of themselves in order to bring beauty and pleasure to others;

To my teachers and professional colleagues, who help facilitate my self-discoveries, and who believe in my potentials;

To E.M., S.J., B.K., and others, who helped define my role as a performing artist and therapist;

To Angelica Petrides, my good friend, who continually makes me feel as if I know what I'm saying;

To Barbara Hesser, Director of the Music Therapy Program at New York University, whose challenges broadened my views of music in therapy;

To composer Donald Erb, whose music has made a difference in my life, and to Lucille Erb, a very special lady;

To Dr. Daniel Schneck, whose incredible scientific and musical intellect helps amalgamate my knowledge into expanded points of view, and to Judith Schneck, whose work as a violinist and teacher inspires my work with musicians;

To my daughters, Carylin and Sabrina, who are and will always be the music in my life;

And, to my husband Larry, the best proofreader around, whose support encourages me to grow.

Introduction

The man, the art, the work—it is all one. The art of the inner work, which unlike the outer does not forsake the artist, which he does not "do" and can only "be", springs from depths of which the day knows nothing.
—Eugene Herrigel,
Zen in the Art of Archery

I have been a classical pianist most of my life. But it was only after I entered the music therapy program at NYU and began researching the *why* of music that I asked: If music has such healing powers, then why aren't musicians the healthiest people around?

Through my own processes in the NYU program, especially in free improvisation classes and groups, and my readings of Zen philosophy, I came to suspect that there may be a missing link somewhere in the preparation of the musician.

My training was conservatory-based, performance (product)-oriented skills training. Most of my time was spent drilling on scales, arpeggios, chords, and being told how to phrase, use dynamics, and understand my instructor's interpretation of the music. But, what about *me*, the person through whom the music would be recreated? *I* was not part of the training. Had obsession with product deprived me of process?

I was luckier than most. Many of my instructors at least made me aware of what my body was doing as I played. It was not until I had the opportunity to be musically explorative and inventive in improvising music for dance improvisation classes that I learned of inner and unconscious creative impulses—the person within the art. Later, when I performed composer Donald Erb's partially aleatoric music, which was improvisatory in nature and played on a specially prepared piano to obtain unusual sounds, I began to have fun with music and the piano. I noticed I was losing performance anxieties; disconnecting from obsessions with technique and perfectionism; dispelling judgments of teachers, friends, family, competitors, and audiences; and making cognitive connections between my self and my music.

Through improvisation, I discovered my Zen being, those moments of peak experiences when my mind, body, spirit, all that I was, am, and can be, united as one in the music. I explored pure expression. There was no room for judgment. I discovered new relationships between myself and the instrument, developed a sense of oneness with the piano and the music, and self-confidence in my intuitions. I redirected my self-discoveries into my solo and chamber music repertoire. Those peak performance moments surpassed technique, analysis and judgment; they went beyond physical space and time to a level of consciousness where the only reality was the breath of my self-expression within the evolving musical thoughts that permeated the inner spaces of my mind and body. These were moments of transcendence, when nothing mattered but the music.

Given my own experiences with free improvisation and what I learned in improvisation groups in the music therapy program at New York University, I asked: If free improvisation in the process of music therapy helps nonmusicians, wouldn't it be all the more powerful as therapy for the musician already well versed in music? And, if the primary instrument were the focus of free improvisation therapy, could the process and working with a music therapist evolve a performer's better sense of confidence, self, and dynamic performance—a unity of mind-body-spirit in performance, when performer and music are one? A Zen of performance?

I decided to combine the music therapy process with my interest in helping young performers to blossom emotionally and psychologically and to develop self-confidence and peak performance experiences. I have been working with instrumentalists and vocalists who have difficulties being fully open and expressive in their music, and who complained of performance anxieties limiting their potential. This book is based on my work with three musicians. Two of them, E.M., a twenty-three-year-old male violist, and S.J., a twenty-year-old female violinist, were attending a prominent New York City conservatory. The third, B.K., was a thirteen-year-old male pianist.

Discussed here are ideas about free improvisation therapy as a modality in music therapy for the performer. My terms "free improvisation therapy" and "music improvisation therapy" throughout this book refer to the kind of music material used in the therapy process of self-expression, disclosure, analysis, and cognition to help clients hear who they are and explore blocks and fears. The client's ongoing process of producing music on his or her instrument, combined with verbal cognitive processing, sustains a familiar and safe environment for unveiling and articulating feelings and issues through music. As a final stage of the therapy process, insights and discoveries are redirected into the repertoire which is being prepared for performance. It is a therapy process employing the individual's instruments and creative musical and analytical skills toward establishing a better sense of self, musicianship, confidence, and concentration.

Explored are issues of creativity and the implication of neurosis upon it; the performer and his or her role; the performance event; music improvisation therapy application for the performer, the music, and the art of performance. This is just the beginning. I am excited about the healing possibilities which music improvisation therapy holds for performers in the future. It is a unique contribution to the development of the whole musician—one who can live the music and reach the peak without fear.

Chapter 1

Creativity and the Performer

When Man learns how to free his creative processes from the drag and bias of covert, neurotic influences, he will have achieved the highest degree of spiritual freedom and the greatest cultural advance of which human nature is capable. He will stand at the frontier of a wholly new land of Canaan.
—Lawrence Kubie
Neurotic Distortion of the Creative Process

SPEAKING OF CREATIVITY

I remember, during undergraduate days, embarking on heated debates with fellow composers about whether or not the performer was a creative artist. Student composers argued that creative artists were those whose ideas were their own—who created the works, such as composers, visual artists, poets, and writers. Performers, they claimed, were not speaking their own ideas but only communicating those of others. Obviously, I stood in disagreement with this myopic view, for without the performer's creative ability to interpret the composer's hieroglyphics, could a composition be communicated at all, other than by the composer performing it? Was not the performer creating meaning and communicating this on behalf of the composer? The arguments never resolved, and I never acquiesced. I have since found support for my position.

Rollo May affirms that "creativity is a necessary sequel to being." By that very definition, the performer, in being, is creative. He further states that creativity is the process of "bringing something new into being... of giving birth to a new reality" (May 1975, 38). For the performer, creativity and music *are* his or her being. The performer is creating new realities out of existing abstract symbols, breathing life into a compendium of dots and lines.

May further distinguishes between talent and creativity, suggesting that the first thing to note about creativity is that it is an encounter—with the moment, the thought, the need, the landscape, the sound, the object, the experience of life. Creativity is the combination of talent for (intuition), and encounter with (action), the object or process. Talent, being more than exhibitionism is the inborn, instinctive ability to see, to connect with, and to give meaning to the encounter. Creativity is manifest in the act of employing talent within encounter.

"Talent may well have its neurological correlates and can be studied as 'given' to a person. A man or woman may have talent whether he or she uses it or not; talent can probably be measured in the person as such. But *creativity* can be seen only in the act" (ibid., 43).

Sometimes we have great talent and simultaneously great encounter, resulting in exceptional creativity, as with Picasso. Sometimes, we have great talent and unrealized creativity (as with artists who never fully actualize); sometimes we even have great creativity but not much talent. It is the clear balance between talent and encounter which defines creativity.

The talented performer, then, is endowed with inborn talent and is creative in the manner in which he or she employs this talent in encountering the instrument and music symbols. By being fully present in the act of discovering, he or she devises something new for the world in the presentation.

"Creativity," according to Lawrence Kubie, "implies invention." He defines creativity as the application of old or new facts and principles, or combinations thereof to the uncovering of even newer facts and newer combinations of ideas, and the amalgamation into new patterns, data whose interdependence may have, hitherto, gone unnoted and unused. "It is this which is common to all creativeness" (Kubie 1961, 50).

Creativity is the shaking up of ideas, memories, feelings, and learned knowledge in the great melting pot of one's experience, and then superimposing conscious intelligence in the process of selecting from among them combinations of patterns that yield new and previously unthought of meaning and significance. In the arts, states Kubie, "cogito" shakes things up, and "the process [of] 'intelligo' tests the creative products for their communicability both as intellectual and as emotional experiences" (ibid., 52). Thus the talented performer creates a new approach to the music.

Abraham H. Maslow defines creativity as the inherent human drive toward self-actualization and attainment of one's full human potential. His theories suggest that creativity, combining learned and experienced data, ultimately manifests itself in the manner in which the human being attains peak experiences. Maslow further states that:

> The creative person, in the inspirational phase of the creative furor, loses his past and his future and lives only in the moment. He is all there, totally immersed…

by the here-now, with the matter-in-hand.... This ability to become "lost in the present" seems to be a sine qua non for creativeness of any kind... [the] ability to become timeless, selfless, outside of space, of society, of history (Maslow 1971, 59).

Indeed, the performer lives only in the moment as sounds emanate moment-to-moment from the instrument. It is only in the present, as a temporal art form, that music can exist. It only has past and future in that it will be compressed into the immediate present and disappear. The performer's creativity is in the unfolding of the present, the moment-to-moment responses discharging tonal and emotional energies toward the listener.

These definitions support the notion that the performer is a creative artist. It could be that instrumental training has omitted psychological nurturing and development of the performer due to resistance in recognizing him as a creative artist equal to the composer. This could be an underlying reason for such stronger emphasis on training only the performer's technical skills (Havas, 1973).

NEUROSIS, CREATIVITY, AND THE PERFORMER

I recall lively discussions about anxiety and neuroses as being necessary evils that enhance creative endeavors. I was often told that without nervousness, my performance would lack a certain vitality and somehow suffer from passivity. Well, I am not sure. Some theories hold the opposite to be true.

I never experienced stage fright—the kind of paralyzing fear precluding the ability to get the job done. I have been nervous—rather anxious and anticipatory about getting on with the performance—but it has been more a feeling of excitement than worry. Nevertheless, anxiety is part of the performer's territory. Anxieties about being less than technically perfect have been programmed into the training aspects of the performer, especially now in the age of high technology, when obsession with technical perfection is rampant.

We live in a world that has become mechanized to the highest degree ever known to man. The problem is that "mechanization requires uniformity, predictability, and orderliness" (May 1975, 75). These are antithetical to creativity that inherits fallibility in trial and error. In fact, the unconscious phenomena of originality and irrationality of the creative spirit, which can as easily impart imperfect impulses along with superior ones, are a threat to order and uniformity. Could this be why people in our modern Western civilization have been afraid of unconscious and irrational experience? "For the potentialities that surge up in [the artist] from deeper mental wells simply don't fit the technology which has become so essential for our world" (ibid., 76).

According to May, ever since the Renaissance, Western civilization "has centrally emphasized techniques and mechanics" (ibid.). But our technology, rather than increasing creativity, has actually blocked it, and our artists are being stifled by what May describes as the "creativity of the spirit." The recording industry has virtually stripped the music audience of the vitality and humanistic quality of creative expression by synthesizing and rendering the performance to be free from error, to the point where human interaction—the communication of performer and audience—has been sterilized out of the recording.

Another factor producing anxiety for today's performer is the obsessive need to have prodigies who attain their training largely by methods employing imitative/rote processes. In rushing technical training and prowess through processes that exclude consideration of psychological developmental growth, it is possible that ultimate anxiety during the transition stages of development can result.

Howard Gardner discusses the musical development of child prodigies and observes that the clash between figural and formal modes of processing may

> occasion a crisis in the lives of young musicians.... Children treated by their communities as prodigies often advance quite far on the basis of figural apprehension of music. At a certain point, however, it becomes important for them to supplement their intuitive understanding with a more systematic knowledge of music lore and law. This bringing-to-consciousness of what was previously assumed (or ignored) can be unsettling for youngsters, particularly for ones who have depended simply upon their intuition, and who may have a resistance to propositional (linguistic or mathematical) characterizations of musical events. The so-called mid-life crisis occurs in the lives of prodigies in adolescence, somewhere between the ages of fourteen and eighteen. If this crisis is not successfully negotiated, it may ultimately prompt the child to cease altogether participating in musical life (Gardner 1983, 111).

For the prodigy especially, but as well for the musically gifted young child, for whom much applause and recognition was given, what was once a process of sheer talent and energy soon requires serious practice.

This transition may have a lasting negative impact upon the development of socialization skills, may become isolating for the adolescent and young adult, and may be a major source of emotional blocking and conflict between the performer and parents/teachers/mentors. In addition, the pressure to be continually brilliant can produce fear, a loss of self-confidence, or mistrust of one's ability to live up to expectations, and an unsettling relationship between the performer and the world (ibid.).

Contrary to folkloric beliefs that neuroses are necessary for creativity, Lawrence Kubie poses an emphatic hypothesis that although neurotic and creative processes are equally ubiquitous, neuroses are *limitations* to creativity rather than necessary evils. He calls it a "culturally noxious assumption, devoid... of the least fragment of truth, that one must be sick to be creative" (Kubie 1961, 4).

Kubie continues with the premise that many psychologically ailing artists, writers, musicians, and scientists, even including some individuals whose productivity may have been seriously impeded by their neuroses, refuse therapy out of fear—fear that in losing their illness they will lose not only their much prized individuality but also their creative zeal and spark. Instead of stressing their creativity, it is implied that it is the artists' neuroses that make them unique. "Yet in reality, the neurosis is the most banal and undistinguished component of human nature" (ibid., 5).

In fact, this underlying but erroneous belief that neurosis is necessary for creativity has created an element of resistance among music professionals toward seeking any kind of therapy. In a recent conversation with an instructor at a prominent conservatory, I suggested conducting some free improvisation sessions for her students, to which she responded, "My dear, our students don't have performance anxiety, or any other kinds of problems related to performance. Our students are experienced professionals!"

Kubie would respond that "the role of neurosis in human life is at once the most pressing yet the least acknowledged challenge which confronts human culture... that the creative spirit today is struggling blindly and confusedly to accept this challenge, and that consequently all of art and literature today deal with the neurotic in human nature." But, he firmly maintains, "the fact remains that the processes of illness block and corrupt the creative act" (ibid., 10–11).

Rollo May agrees with Kubie, stating that he "emphatically disagree[s] with the implication that creativity is to be understood by reducing it to... essentially an expression of neurosis" (May 1975, 36). He asks if, by psychoanalysis, we were to cure the artist of his or her neurosis, would the artist no longer create? If the artist creates out of some transfer of affect or drive, as implied in sublimation, or if creativity is merely the by-product of an endeavor to accomplish something else, as in compensation, does not our very creative act then have only a pseudo value? "We must indeed take a strong stand against the implications, however they may creep in, that talent is a disease and creativity is a neurosis" (ibid., 37).

May suggests that anxiety is a natural state in creative being, preceding the unknown of one's changing relationship with his world and that the anxiety dissipates once the artist is fully within the act of creating. Paralleled in the performer would be the anxiety preceding performance—the unknown—that, once embarked upon, develops into a controllable and comfortable known.

Kubie summarizes that the preconscious is "the essential implement of all creative activity and that unless preconscious processes can flow freely there can be no true creativity" (Kubie, 1961, 137). "The preconscious does not function alone but in balance with the symbolic process of the conscious—the symbols of which we fully understand—and the symbolic process of the unconscious—the symbolic meanings of which, although we are conscious of them, elude us, are unknown and inaccessible except by special methods of exploration."

The balance between these three poles: conscious, preconscious, and unconscious, results in the highest form of creativity and the highest form of normal behavior. Dominance of any of the poles results in distortion of affect, blocks to creativity, and other interfering disabilities (ibid.). For the performer, such blocks can result in stilted, stiff performances, fear of expression and self-discovery, and possibly an inability to relate to or communicate with the audience.

Creativity means working freely with the conscious and preconscious metaphor; with slang, puns, overlapping meanings, and figures of speech; with vague similarities; with the reminiscent recollections evoked by some minute ingredients of experience, establishing links to something else that in other respects may be quite different. "It [creativity] is free in the sense that it is not anchored either to the pedestrian realities of our conscious symbolic processes, or to the rigid symbolic relationships of the unconscious areas of the personality" (ibid., 141).

Abraham Maslow stands alongside May and Kubie in regarding neuroses and blocks as detrimental to creativity and full self-actualization. He alleges that although anxiety is territorial to creativity and results from movement toward the unknown, the myth that neurotic behavior is part and parcel of creativity is a fallacy. He also suggests that removal of blocks, neuroses, and psychological interferences frees the creative being to pursue complete self-actualization.

Maslow calls for the balance of conscious and unconscious processes in order to achieve full potential and states that "in the healthy person, and especially the healthy person who creates, I find that he has somehow managed a fusion and a synthesis of both primary and secondary processes; both conscious and unconscious; both of deeper self and of conscious self" (Maslow 1971, 85).

The performer could have developed blocks and neuroses throughout developmental stages, originating in part from the rigors of current trends in instrumental training that seem to exclude humanism and nurturing of the being. These problems could restrict the free-flowing expression required in music performance. The audience, the receiver of music communication, would be implicated as well. After all, as Kubie reminds us, "The toll which neurosis exacts of Man's creative potential is paid by all human culture" (Kubie 1961, 6).

One measure of health is flexibility. "The essence of normality is flexibility... the essence of illness is the freezing of behavior into unalterable and insatiable patterns.... Any moment of behavior is neurotic if the processes that set it in motion predetermine its automatic repetition" (ibid., 21).

Flexibility as normal behavior requires a balance between the conscious, preconscious, and unconscious processes. The performer operates "in the shadow of illness whenever unconscious processes are dominant" (ibid., 22), rendering instinct and cognition basically inflexible to new patterns of intuition. Blocks and neuroses, rather than being assets, become detrimental to the performer's creativity.

Alleviation of blocks could result in a healthier balance between the conscious, preconscious, and unconscious symbolic processes required in order to be fully flexible and creative. Reducing blocks and neuroses would enable the performer to become more flexible, to draw upon his or her talent in more fully exploring the creative potential, and to employ creativity freely in attaining self-actualization as a person and performer. It could help in the process of realizing those dynamic performance peaks that are the goals of every performer.

In working improvisationally, E.M. (viola) heard the sounds and sensed bodily impulses created by the sounds of his repressed anger. Exploring these musically not only helped him find relief and possible resolution but also self-confidence in his creative abilities to make music without needing to be technically perfect. Through improvisation, S.J. (violin) sought to broaden her emotional spectrum of self-expression. What did talking back to authority feel like, musically? What happened to her body? Her mind? Her music? Where in the repertoire would she need this kind of self-expression? Why were these blocked? B.K. (piano) felt totally useless, a word assigned to him by his father. "Can't do it" permeated his thoughts. But, what if he could do anything he wanted to on the piano? What would he express? How would he assert himself? What would he say to his father, musically? How did his father make him feel? What did those feelings sound like? Which of those feeling sounds were required by Bartók? Was Bartók a version of his father? Was the piano a symbol for validating his father's opinion?

E.M., S.J., and B.K. are talented artists with creative abilities to apply their talents toward recognition and discovery of new alternatives that, through application of learned skills, culminate in refreshing new choices and dynamic results. They have been exploring their issues through the creative process of discovering their own inner music and playing the music of others with new found expressivity.

As clients discover and become confident with their infinite creative potential, there develops increased incentives for further musical and personal explorations. Discoveries are reinvested into new relationships with musical repertoire and expressed outwardly through performance.

Chapter 2

The Role of Performer, the Act of Performance

In the art of music, creation and interpretation are indissolubly linked... both these activities demand an imaginative mind.
—Aaron Copland
Music and Imagination

THE ROLE OF PERFORMER

Having established that the performer is a creative artist, I turn my investigation to the role of the performer, which parallels that of an actor.

My role as performer, in preparing and communicating the musical thoughts of someone else is that of co-composer, collaborator, co-creator. For it is I who ultimately interprets the written symbols and directions into sound; I infuse these with my own sense of self and universe—my understanding of and relationship with the world, my technical skill in translating the composer's intention, and my ability to unite with and conform to the composer's emotional energy. It is I who gives reality to, who acts out, the composer's musical (illusory) train of thought; it is I who "'concretizes' the [composer's musical] myth," as Joseph Campbell might suggest (Campbell 1988).

Roger Sessions reminds us that originally composer, performer, and listener were one being. Primitive cultures created, played, and were audience to their own music making. "Music was vocal or instrumental improvisation" (Sessions 1950, 4) related to rituals and festivals in which whole communities participated. It was not until later in social development, when certain patterns

9

of musical expression became fixed traditions needing to be reproduced more than once in the same way, that the functions of composer and performer became differentiated.

According to Sessions, "The first performer was, in the strictest sense, the first musician who played or sang something that had been played or sung before... who first sang music composed by someone other than himself." However, Sessions insists, this separation between composer and performer in no way obscures "the fact that in the last analysis composer and performer are not only collaborators in a common enterprise but participants in an essentially single experience" (ibid., 5).

I became fully aware of this co-creator role when I worked improvisationally with composer Donald Erb in Cleveland's Multi-Media Theater. He presented me with few notated symbols. He spoke of possibilities, concepts of sounds—clusters in various registers, frantic runs and arpeggiated passages not key-centered, white (nontonal) sound, clanging and chiming sounds to be attained through prior preparation of the piano strings that would later be struck by mallets and various implements, and so on. The impulse and inner understanding of the music, rhythm, phrasing, overall dynamics, and intensities were my contribution according to my creative flexibility, piano skills, understanding of the medium, and my personal connection with the composer's being in the music I was to represent.

Although I was actually improvising (composing) the music as I played, I realized whether I read written symbols or was verbally told what the composer heard in his head, the final process of rendering the musical thought was the same. I ultimately created what the audience heard, acting as the composer as much as I was the performer. His energies blended with mine; his musical thoughts became enhanced by mine; I heard through his imagination; he heard through mine. But had I been *trained* to do this? To think this way? No.

A dilemma of today's musician, Don Erb would complain, is that the musician has no contact with contemporary notation. It is a foreign language that most musicians cannot, nor want to, learn to decipher. Fortunately, some performers at least have absorbed the intensities and psyche of our own contemporary culture, enabling them almost by rote, to infuse understanding and authenticity into today's sonorous metaphors. But performers in the next century may be no better prepared psychologically and emotionally to project the music of today's composers than I was to project the music of past centuries, if notation-centered technical training continues as is.

Donald Erb's dilemma underscores my belief that just as an actor assumes aspects of his character, the performer, by deciphering a map of symbols, inflections, and tonal contours leading to a plethora of possible outcomes, temporarily assumes the role, personality, and mind of the composer, nearly becoming his contemporary, in order to create, as a *re*-creation, his own musical train of thought.

"The performer, then, must discover according to his abilities the composer's intentions and project them according to his own conviction" emphasizes Roger Sessions (ibid., 82). But, he asks, is the performer merely a medium for transmitting the composer's intentions according to his or her technical capacities and skills in deciphering the text? No. The *performer's* intentions are also heard in the music.

Many composers, including Sessions, Copland, and Stravinsky, agree that music notation, despite all the efforts on the composer's part to translate his wishes and intentions, can never be exact, just as words in a drama script cannot exactly reflect the intentions and feelings of the character who recites them. "In projecting the work, the performer has to exercise individual judgment at many points" (Sessions 1950, 82). Herein lies what Aaron Copland refers to as "the interaction between the creative and the interpretative mind" (Copland 1952, 57). Copland sees the musician's role as greater than the actor's. "One might almost maintain that musical interpretation demands of the performer an even wider range [of inner comprehension] than that of the actor, because the musician must play every role in the piece" (ibid., 58).

The performer's role is to identify not only the intellectual, emotional, and psychological processes and intentions of the composer (conscious, preconscious, and unconscious process referred to in Chapter 1) but also his own. It is by resonating with the composer on a level beyond the symbols on a page that the performer becomes most unified, most identified, with the being of the composer. "Composers of all times have demanded of performers whatever liveliness and eloquence the latter could give. They have not… attempted to indicate the intangible factors in the performance… these factors, which make all the difference… between a good performance and a bad one, cannot conceivably be indicated in any score" (Sessions 1950, 73).

Just as an actor brings a character to life, the performer brings the composer to life through his presentation of the music. The performer blends his or her being with that of the composer, taking on similar characteristics, sensations, musical trains of thought, in order to authentically and faithfully represent the composer's central ideas. In a sense, the music becomes incorporated into the performer's being, and emanates forth to the audience as a blend of both composer and performer.

Therefore, it seems logical that in addition to the rigors of technical instrumental training the instrumentalist needs preparation and training similar to that of the actor: sensitivity training that fully explores emotional responses, role characterization, dynamic use of the body as part of the performing instrument, and improvisational exploration of spontaneity such as games, self-awareness, etc. (Spolin 1963, Balk 1991). Sensitivity training subsumes becoming cognizant of one's self in relation to self; to others (i.e., composer and audience); and objects, musical instruments, media, etc.; and learning to freely project these to the audience.

One of the games I played with violinist S.J., prior to working with her on the emotions needed for the Tchaikovsky *Violin Concerto*, was similar to a musical relay. I would begin an improvisation on the piano. When she felt ready, she would pick it up on her violin and imitate it as closely as possible in terms of qualities, energies, syntax, ranges, rhythms, etc. After accepting the musical idea as I had presented it on the piano, she could begin to transform it into something of her own. When I was ready, I would take her music, reflect it as she had done when she took the music from me, and then I transformed it. After six or seven musical exchanges, upon receiving a cue from me, we would continue playing together whichever improvisation happened to be the final one.

When we ended, she was asked to share her feelings and experiences. This game often seemed to result in disturbances. S.J. related the resistance of certain feelings and images which she felt emanated from some of the improvisations she took from me: feelings of agitation or fear, being chased, ugly sound, and so on. My musical interventions had been purposely ones of feelings I knew S.J. would be resistant to exploring on her own. Her responses were not unexpected.

Her strongest feelings and issues would then become material for further improvisational explorations, for instance her feeling of being chased explored several different endings: her catching me, my catching her, both running away from or toward each other, and one hiding from the other. Discussions of feelings, issues, and the music continued to reveal discomfort levels.

Eventually, S.J. could identify some of the emotions and sensations she had been suppressing, recall them and repeat them in other improvisations. Several meetings featuring these improvisational sequences occurred before she could become comfortable identifying the emotions within herself and the Tchaikovsky Concerto, and be less frightened of expressing them.

Another music improvisation game I played with each client was what I call "Emotions A to Z." The objective was to call out an emotion, mood, judgment, or object for each letter of the alphabet, Anger, Bad, Cute, Danger, etc., before the client's or my turn to start the improvisation. Each duet improvisation defining the item was to last two to three minutes and come to resolution. Sometimes the item would be called out first, followed by the musical definition. At other times, just the letter would be called out, followed by the music, and the identity of the item would be guessed at by either the client or myself, depending on whose definition was being played.

At times this game served as a warm-up, using six or eight alphabet letters. There was often disagreement about musical qualities representing the items. Ensuing discussions usually provided the clients with clues and insights about themselves. My role was to be true to my own individual musical idea, rather than reflecting or supporting that of the client. This fostered a look at issues of similarities and differences between the client and the therapist, the client and the composer, the client and others in his or her life. In identifying feelings, the client could learn about the basic beliefs and boundaries he or she had established for himself or herself. This exercise revealed degrees of comfort and discomfort with individuality, convictions about feelings, and issues of trust in one's own creative instincts.

The role of the performer is to realize the essence of the composer within the music and within him or her, infusing the music with the sensibilities, intuitions and awareness of himself or herself, the composer, and the music. The performer acts out in sound those inner thoughts and impulses that the composer called upon to project creative energies. The performer must do this without losing his or her own boundaries or sense of personal reality and being. This is precisely why a strong, developed sense of self is so important for the performer.

THE PERFORMANCE

The roles of the performer and composer become quite irrelevant unless there is an opportunity to share the experience and communicate musical thoughts with an audience. The listener is the ultimate target of all that precedes.

It is at this point that the instrumentalist undergoes a metamorphosis from practice-room technician to onstage musician. The performance is born. Keeping his or her goals firmly in the forefront of consciousness, "it is at this moment that the performer's attention turns from problem-solving (making something go away, such as technical problems) to creating (making something come into being—the music)" (Robert Fritz, cited in Balk 1991, 177).

Maintaining a clear vision of the task at hand, the performer begins to move into the realm of the unknown and must have complete confidence in the ability not only to deliver the music but to sense the audience and assess the circumstances in which the music will be imparted.

The performance scenario itself is a dynamic system of interactions and interdependencies often looming larger than the performance act itself. Figure 1 demonstrates some of the main factors, internal and external, characterizing and affecting the performance. It was designed with the solo performer in mind, but can be applied in this simple form to duo performers or soloist and accompanist, who function together as one unit. Not discussed here are the more complex performances involving soloists with orchestras that include dynamics of conductors and a 106-member ensemble; larger instrumental ensembles (unless they can be grouped as a single unit); and stage presentations such as operas, oratorios, choral works, etc. In these, obvious additional factors enter into the chart but are not relevant for this discussion.

At the top of the circle in Figure 1 is the Performer—the initiator, or active participant in the act of performance. He or she consists of a total being: mind-body-spirit in the here-and-now situation. Among other things, influencing each performer are training, education, family, culture, life's experiences, and worldview.

Next, as we move clockwise around the circle, is the composer and his or her total being: mind-body-spirit, as it was at the time of the creation of the music (the then present). Among other things, influencing the composer were training, education, family, culture, life's experiences, and worldview.

Figure 1
Factors Functioning in the Performance of Music

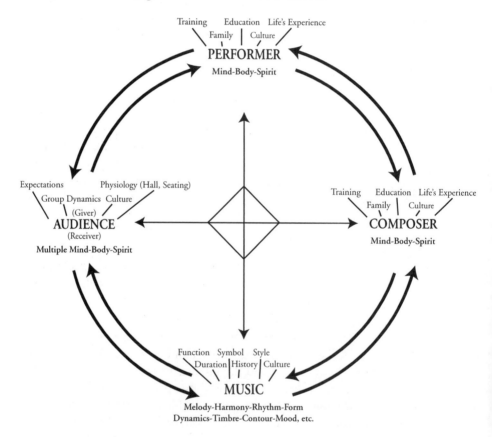

NOTE: *Indications above titles identify some external influences upon factors; indications below titles identify internal influences. The combined elements seem to loom larger than the performance event (the crossroad at center) itself. Therefore, it would appear that the total performance components are greater than the actual moment of performance itself.*

The interaction between composer and performer is often impeded by generation gaps that, at times, can be centuries apart. The wider the gap, the more difficult the task of the performer in bridging and integrating with the music in the present.

The music is the third factor in the performance dynamics. It contains its own being, articulated in its elements of melody, harmony, rhythm, dynamics, tempo, timbre (often complicated by the presence of more than one instrument), form, overall contour, mood, emotion, architecture, and more. Influencing the music, in addition to the composer's impulse, is its function and purpose, its symbols, style, duration, history, and culture from which it emanated.

Fourth, we have the audience factor, its being comprised of its multiple-personality-parts of mind-body-spirit, and its dual role as (a) receiver of the music: hearing ability, musical cognition, etc. and (b) giver to the performer: attention, demeanor, opinion, appreciation, etc. As with the other elements, the audience is also influenced in part by its expectations, group dynamics, concert hall and seating arrangement, plus the time and duration of performance.

The listener (audience) to the music essentially follows a performance by recreating it in his or her own mind. The listener actually performs it in his or her own imagination, by remembering and recreating it as it is being produced. "He really listens precisely to the degree that he does this, and really hears to precisely the extent that he does it successfully" (Sessions 1950, 8).

These four major aspects interact in a circular motion, each element influencing the other in both directions around the circle. Thus, the performer and his or her internal and external influences impact upon the composer by reinterpreting his or her music and his or her influences, and vice versa; the composer impacts upon the music which impacts upon the composer; the music impacts upon the audience, and the audience impacts upon the music through its cognitive relationship with it; the audience impacts on the performer who impacts upon the audience.

Finally, in addition to the circular influences, there is a cross connection between the four major elements: the performer directly connects with the music that enables the audience to have a direct connection with the composer. For the listener, the "ideal aim is to apprehend to the fullest and most complete possible extent the musical utterance of the composer as the performer delivers it to him" (ibid.).

It is the center of the performance circle, the meeting point or cross section of the four elements, that defines the peak of the actual performance. It is this intersection that unites all the elements, or that gives birth to the larger whole.

The factors in Figure 1 demonstrate the broad scope of interactive elements that the performer must synthesize into his or her awareness—far exceeding merely the technical production of the music. A performance must be accepted as a major social ceremony that is "both an exposition of the piece and an exposition of the personality traits of the performer" (Copland 1952, 61). Musical authenticity is expected by the audience, demanding the performer's full presence not only onstage but in the emotional state of the music being projected out to the community of listeners.

For the performer, the prismatic performance ritual provides the maximum opportunity to attain self-actualization on the continuum of musical potential—the dynamic vibrancy of which would be equivalent to Maslow's "peak experience" (Maslow 1970). It is onstage where the final, complete balance and interplay between discipline and freedom takes place; where the greatest vitality occurs (Balk 1991).

Chapter 3

Improvisation in Music Therapy and the Performer

All right doing is accomplished only in a state of true selflessness, in which the doer cannot be present any longer as "himself." Only the spirit is present, a kind of awareness which shows no trace of egohood and for that reason ranges without limit through all distances and depths, with "eyes that hear and with ears that see."

—Eugene Herrigel
Zen in the Art of Archery

SPEAKING OF IMPROVISATION

The *Harvard Dictionary of Music* defines improvisation and extemporization, as "The art of performing music as an immediate reproduction of simultaneous mental processes, that is, without the aid of manuscript, sketches, or memory." Of special interest is the further description of improvisation as "a 'soap-bubble' phenomenon the evanescent nature of which defies documentation and detailed description" (Apel 1968, 351).

Jacques-Dalcroze, founder of the Eurhythmics Improvisation approach to learning music, addressed improvisation as "the study of direct relations between cerebral commands and muscular interpretations in order to express one's own musical feelings.... Performance is propelled by developing the students' powers of sensation, imagination, and memory" (Abramson 1980, 64).

French philosopher Henri Bergson hypothesized that human intuition was a way of obtaining direct contact with a prime reality that might otherwise be obscured from human knowledge. Seeing intuition as special insight to experience,

Bergson felt that human intellect could freely interact with constructs emanating from one's intuition to develop an enriched personal perspective (Bergson, 1959). "The notion of tapping a prime reality [through intuition] is very similar to the improviser's aesthetic of tapping the flow of the music" (Pressing 1988, 148).

I define free improvisation as an intuitive, expressive invention of free-flowing musical trains of thought, following no prescribed order, containing no specifically preordered form or tonality, and employing musical elements derived through random-impulse selection of the moment. It differs from jazz improvisation that encompasses a preestablished harmonic and rhythmic structure within which thematic variations are freely extemporized. Like the evanescent soap bubble, free improvisation provides an immediate glimpse into the rainbow of emotional and psychological states of mind of the being in the here-and-now.

Free improvisation using a wide range of percussive instruments is a frequently employed technique in music therapy, and is a predominant modality with non-musician populations who are psychiatrically or developmentally debilitated (Nordoff and Robbins 1977, Priestley 1975, Boxill 1985, Alvin 1965, 1978). It is used to achieve relatedness (Stephens 1983) between client and therapist, client and instruments, members in a group setting, and often, between the client and his or her inner being. It is employed in efforts to discover and communicate with the inner being and includes techniques of musical reflection, synchronicity, techniques of being a role model, grounding, instigation and musical engagement of patients and clients.

The ability to embark on free improvisation in music therapy is seen as a necessary competence for the music therapist (Bruscia, Hesser, and Boxill 1981) and is used widely within the field, both in group and individual therapy. My course work in musical therapy included musical styles improvisation, and both instrumental and vocal free improvisation techniques. Many music therapists employ free improvisation, both instrumental and vocal, in tandem with specific verbal psychology theories in working with higher functioning clients to reach repressed emotions and derive resolution to psychological conflicts (Austin 1986).

FREE IMPROVISATION MUSIC THERAPY FOR THE PERFORMER

In reviewing the chapters on creativity and the performer, the role of performer, and the formidable task of performance, it is no wonder that anxieties are part and parcel of the performer's territory. Fortunately for some, the mental and emotional factors of performance have been well integrated, psychologically, and have not impeded upon self-expression or self-confidence. These performers present themselves and the music with full confidence. They are secure with themselves, their training, and the audience; are at one with the music; and usually possess nerves of steel.

For a great many others of equal talent and skills, the demands for technical perfection, the fragile young age at which instrumental studies were begun, cultural obsession with early achievement, and other determinants have resulted in insecurities, fears of failure and rejection, paralyzing perfectionist syndromes, loss of confidence, and frustration. These problems, coupled with existing repressed emotions and the clinging to old habits and thought processes, tend to delimit full musical and personal potential.

Music improvisation therapy, especially as part of the musical development process of the performer, is the most direct therapeutic intervention to address the problems of the musical being as a person and as a musician. "The art of improvisation rests on… a developed awareness of one's expressive individuality" (Doerschuk 1984, 52). This knowledge can grow through interactive and solo improvisational experiences between the performer and the music therapist, whose function it is to pose questions intended to provoke personal and musical insight.

B.K. (piano), for example, harbored an intense fear of failure. On the other hand, his failure would validate his father's opinion of him: that he was totally useless. B.K.'s father, a dentist, once expressed this opinion to me in B.K.'s presence. This cycle could maintain the father as being right, so that B.K. could continue believing in his father's omnipotence. However, as important as it seemed to B.K. to succeed at failing, it was becoming just as important at this age of thirteen to fourteen that he be academically and socially acceptable, not failing.

Until we started improvisation and music therapy, I sensed B.K. felt comfortable using the piano as his failure symbol, while he excelled in science. At first, it was uncomfortable for B.K. to improvise. He may have feared actually being good at it. I thought of him as extremely inventive and creative. We met for one hour every week, during which time I was directive in asking him to explore improvisational tasks that could help illuminate some of his issues.

My initial interest was in exploring his interaction and relationship with his instrument, the piano. What was the piano, to him? He responded that the piano was something his father had wanted to learn. I asked what he thought of piano sounds. He shrugged. Our first several sessions were devoted to having him explore piano sounds and playing improvised duets with me, in which I could provide role models for ideas, and support and reflect some of his. Our discussions dealt mainly with his inability to learn music and his assumption that he was ill suited for the piano.

During our fourth session, I suggested that B.K. pretend to be a great concert pianist, playing on the stage of a huge concert hall. I would be the audience, and he could add any other phantom audience members he wished. He could play anything he wanted to invent, in any style. B.K. became giddy, but he agreed. I sat across the room and held a piece of paper, pretending it was a program. He came into the room from the hallway. I applauded politely, and he bowed, sat down and waited. His eyes were focused on the keyboard.

There was silence. He slowly lifted both his arms, and let them drop on the keyboard, creating a thundering chord cluster which he held, pedaled, and allowed to resonate. Then, more thundering chords were played with both hands. They were heavy, resounding, forte chords, that were pedaled. There were clusters of sounds on each register of the instrument that were resonating. The rhythm involved repetitions that were calculated to be long-short, long-short-short, long, short-short-short, both hands spread apart on different registers, and alternating between playing in contrary and parallel motion.

He continued improvising for some five to six minutes, seemingly completely drawn to the resonating sounds. He resolved by playing repeating long chord clusters, beginning at the bottom of the piano and working his way to the top, allowing the final chords to resonate until the sound faded into inaudibility. His hands fell to his lap. He continued to stare at the keyboard. I applauded and yelled "Bravo." He smiled, stood up, bowed, and sat down again, beaming. He said it was a sonata for his father. He resented his father's opinion, and as he played, he thought of all the ways in which he would tell his father how badly he felt. Then he became frightened, and at the end, realized he was not really ready to tell his father what he felt. Thus, he said, he allowed his "anger to leave from the top of the keyboard to the sky."

In subsequent improvisations, when we played duets, I sat at the high register of the keyboard, reflecting, holding, and providing a role model in possible ways for him to express his anger and needs without "leave from the top of the keyboard." Together we musically and verbally explored other aspects of those repressed angry feelings: fear, in the form of "jitters every time dad comes home," appearing as staccato black notes; frustration at continually asking for, but being denied his father's affection, appearing as repeated two-note dissonances, ultimately unresolved and suddenly abandoned; jealousy, appearing musically as mocking dissonant sounds representing his sneering (his definition) at his two younger brothers, and so on.

As our sessions accumulated, B.K.'s relationship to the piano began changing. He was now so interested in improvising that I opened the grand piano's lid to allow him to pluck, pull and discover other "weird" sounds on the strings. His focus diverted from the piano as the instrument of his *father's* desires, to an instrument of infinite sound potential. The more he enjoyed his creative explorations, the more secure he became about his abilities, and the closer he came to addressing his father directly.

In addition, I assisted him in investing a great deal of his discoveries into several Bartók piano pieces that he previously had difficulty learning. As he grew to understand himself, he became comfortable with the playfulness and dissonances of the Bartók piano pieces and unafraid of making mistakes.

One of the most exciting events for B.K. was when the organizer of his school's science fair asked him to create a tape of background music to be played during the exhibition of science projects. Gathering all his technology and musical creativity, B.K. produced a remarkable tape, including his own piano sounds, and offered to perform a newly learned Bartók piece during a science fair talent show. B.K.'s father phoned me to ask whether I thought B.K. could handle it. I suggested the father ask his son! B.K. performed with full confidence, as he had done during our practice session. The father was confused. B.K. and I still work together.

For the performer, music is already part of daily life. High-level knowledge of musical syntax on the part of both performer and therapist enables full immersion into, and discussion of, the music improvised and the music to be performed, relative to its essence, expressiveness, metaphor, emotion, intensity, and imagery. The degree of comfort with the modality of free improvisation and the predominant use of the performer's own instrument seems a most natural form of therapy for a performer striving toward self-awareness and infusion of that self-awareness into the musicianship component.

This link between the instrumentalist and his music, explored through improvisation as a mechanism for self-discovery, is a new idea. It leaves the field open for music therapists who combine a strong and comprehensive musical background, a knowledge of psychology and clinical training to work with performers.

There is support for using free improvisation as a therapy modality in music therapy. In *Music Therapy in Action* (1975), Mary Priestley devotes attention to a person's "inner music" as indicating one's emotional issues. In the performer, although he or she may not always be aware of it, the manner in which he or she approaches musical expression reflects the performer's personality traits, as Copland reminded us earlier. Discussing improvisation as a means for deriving a being's personal inner music, Priestley adds:

> Inner music is coloured by the residue of unexpressed emotion coming from habitual attitudes, emotional reactions to past events and expectations about the future. It is always there, in everyone, but differs tremendously from person to person. Certain people have a reliable uplifting melody to which one turns in certain moods.... Others live in a poisonous fog of soured, static hate music which destroys and negates everything they come in contact with (Priestley 1975, 200).

Priestley also acknowledges that "for the performer, music composed by other people provides him with useful self-discipline and efforts to attune his emotional pitch to theirs, but affords little help to him in finding his own centre and means of creative expression." Priestley's statement seems to support the need for additional improvisation therapy work, if the performer is fully to discover himself or herself and his own center and emotional pitch through and within music (ibid., 246).

For many musicians, the idea of seeking therapy is often frightening, as Lawrence Kubie suggests in Chapter 1, and is fraught with denial and resistance. Verbal therapy alone can be even more uncomfortable and frightening for performers, who have been conditioned to nonverbal expression. They often feel that their plight cannot be truly understood by those who do not have personal experience in music performance.

Mary Priestley recognizes this stating:

> To one trained to release his feelings in the rich, colourful, nonverbal medium of music, mere talking seems to lack something as a completely satisfactory means of expression; it leaves an uncomfortable physical and emotional residue of the verbally inexpressible (ibid., 247).

Much that can be hidden in words comes forth more directly through music. For instance, feeling angry may require other words to define (or obscure) its energy as the person actually experiences the emotion. However, angry playing can immediately compress all specific sensations related to the word into the ontological manner of the performer's musical expression. Music can generally be indicative of multiple layers of feeling energies expressed in separate but simultaneous musical components: rhythm, tonality, manner of playing, body language, dynamics, facial expressions, duration, and intensity of playing.

Hypothetically, therefore, anger expressed in loud dynamics can still maintain the consonant (rather than dissonant) sonority of major mode indicative of frustrated resolve, accompanied by broad rhythmic patterns. This could be long tones, possibly indicating dread, performed with the body in a slumped position which could indicate lethargy or commitment to anger. Verbally, these aspects of anger would require lengthy explanations, if at all possible. Very often the essence of real sensations felt during the playing of music has no counterpart in verbal description.

On the other hand, music can become a distancing factor behind which the performer attempts to hide true feelings, fearing that to express true feelings fully could erupt in frightening sounds. The trouble is, in *music* one cannot really cover up the fact that one is actually trying to hide, for this is also revealed in the music. It is easier to camouflage with words—and every musician knows this.

It is the music therapist's role to assist the instrumentalist in exploring, recognizing, and becoming confident in himself or herself and his or her impact on the ultimate product of his or her creative goal—the music performance.

Violinist S.J.'s problems were the reverse of those of B.K. When S.J. and I began working, the idea of being less than perfect was not within the realm of possibilities. Her parents, of Far Eastern cultural background, considered S.J. to be utterly perfect in every way. She was a top honors student, diligent in her violin practice habits, accurate to the ultimate degree. She was kind, loving, caring, tolerant, helpful, considerate, beautifully dressed, neatly groomed, always smiling, perfection personified. But S.J.'s range of emotional expression was so limited that she had great difficulty expressing the magnitude of feelings required by violin repertoire (see Chapter 2).

Improvisation sessions with S.J. were weekly, one-and-one-half hours long. At first, these sessions were extremely difficult for S.J. The idea of improvising without guidelines enabling her to play the correct notes was utterly frightening. I accompanied her on the piano during most of our early sessions, enabling her to follow some of the piano ideas, creating playful tasks, such as "hit and run," during which I played a motif that she was to answer with a run of some sort, and vice versa, musical conversations describing our daily routines, and so on. As we played together, I suggested that since I preferred to play atonally rather than key centered, she might seek to explore tonalities that are not key centered, but rather more dissonant, or less predictable, to see what these felt like.

We worked very slowly at first and rarely processed verbally. I allowed her many sessions to explore just being musically inventive, and helped her develop a sense of safety with me and confidence in herself. By the time we had met some six times, she had become quite playful on her violin and during one session, even offered to play the piano for me while I improvised on the violin. This was a most revealing session for her, because she allowed herself to play impulsively anything that came to her mind, anywhere her hands and fingers landed. I followed on the violin and played outrageous sounds and textures all over the fingerboard, and we both broke into laughter. What happened? "It was all so wrong, it was right," she responded. "I felt like I sneezed," she continued, "and my sinuses cleared." From that point on, S.J. allowed herself to play wrong notes and shrug these off with a giggle.

During another session, I asked S.J. to play the ugliest, most horrible sounds she could play on the violin. She was delighted to comply and proceeded to play with the wood of the bow, scratching, holding the fiddle upside down, untuning the strings normally tuned in perfect fifths, and playing 'hit and run' a cappella, laughing all the way.

Her repertoire in training consisted of the Tchaikovsky *Violin Concerto* and the first violin part of a Bartók *String Quartet*, both works requiring passion, extremes of emotional temerity, intense, and at times even ugly sounds. S.J. was becoming better able to play her repertoire, which she demonstrated for me at several sessions, and was exploring the outer limits of her expressivity, releasing her anxious need to be perfect and beautiful for her parents, teachers, and audience. As our work continued, she explored issues that had been too fearful to investigate earlier, and her creative improvisations demonstrated an authenticity and expressive commitment that had originally been missing from her music. She was no longer hiding behind the repertoire as she had been doing prior to our work together.

I am committed to the idea that free improvisation as a main intervention in music therapy can be a direct process through which the performer can investigate his or her psychological problems through his or her own intuitive (improvised) music, and simultaneously reach a new awareness and resolution of his or her musical problems. The cognitive, high-functioning musician, assisted by the music therapist, can analyze, process, and amalgamate new psychological discoveries observed through freely improvised music which may not have been as easily detectable through verbalization or a written piece of repertoire.

This higher state of conscious awareness evolves in a nonthreatening manner, under familiar circumstances of music-making employing a language common to both parties. Once integrated into the conscious self, this newly found material, which may hitherto have been a form of blocked emotional energy, can be imbued directly into the performance repertoire, and steps toward a self-confident performance can begin.

Chapter 4

Free Improvisation Therapy and the Music

I firmly believe that a certain type of instrumental instruction which teaches students first to learn notes and then, as it is quaintly put, to "put in the expression," is not only musically but instrumentally false... espressivo is in the music itself.... It is in the structure of the music and in the last analysis is identical with this structure."

—Roger Sessions
The Musical Experience of Composer,
Performer, Listener

BACKGROUND

There are any number of self-help books addressing performance fears suggesting mental and physical ways to confront body tensions and imagined judgmental voices that disable the performer. Many of these books are written by psychologists who focus on addressing the sources of anxieties, many more are by musicians and teachers sharing their own insights and struggles. Some books which I have perused for this study include *Stage Fright* (Havas 1973), *A Soprano On Her Head* (Ristad 1982), *The Inner Game of Music* (Green & Gallwey 1986), *Never Be Nervous Again* (Sarnoff 1987), *The Performer Prepares* (Caldwell 1990), and *The Radiant Performer* (Balk 1991). Each approach is highly credible and informative and provides a multitude of ideas, exercises, and mind-sets for overcoming performance anxieties. These include visualization techniques, mental performance rehearsals, imaginary conversations with critical voices, physical relaxation and body response activities, and musical games.

Most approaches seem predominantly reminiscent of behavior-modification-based techniques, that can often bypass the integrative synthesis of inner feelings to outer stimulus. Not to decry the validity of self-help approaches to the problem, I submit that the mental lectures one must embark upon in incorporating some of the approaches tend to evaporate in the performance battlefield. I believe a more in-depth approach, such as free improvisation therapy, could impart more long-lasting results.

I am not the first music therapist to express an interest in developing modalities of free improvisation functions in addressing performance anxiety. Louise Montello (1986, 1989) has been investigating this syndrome from physiological and psychological perspectives and has suggested a need for music therapy as part of music training. Her thesis (1986) and dissertation (1989) contain comprehensive reviews of psychological derivatives inducing performance anxiety and stage fright. Montello and Barbara Hesser collaborated in a clinical research project monitoring musicians in group music improvisation sessions conducted over a specified period of time. In *Utilizing Music Therapy as a Mode of Treatment for the Performance Stress of Professional Musicians* (Montello 1989), the investigators report that group music therapy had a positive, observable, and confirmed impact on the performer's sense of self-esteem, musicianship and reduction of performance stress. Ms. Montello deduces that "the results of this exploratory study suggest that the group music therapy treatment approach was effective in reducing the fear/anxiety subcomponent of musical performance stress…" (ibid., 25).

For the research project, Montello (1989) approached the various aspects of performance anxiety from the psychological points of view—the split self, unresolved issues with mother, narcissism, et al. Her findings state that "during the process of group music therapy, subjects …[became] aware of and integrate[d] the split-off feelings underlying their performance anxiety" (ibid., 61). She further observed that as the subjects became more accepting and less judgmental, they also became more musically expressive and were able to take the focus off themselves while performing, giving their music "unselfconsciously to the audience" (ibid.).

Of special interest to me, although not surprising, was the fact that the subjects displayed greater discomfort when they improvised or played on their own instruments than when they used any of the other instruments. This implies that there exists important psychological and musical issues involving the performer's relationship with his or her instrument as an object and as a vehicle for making music as noted in the previous example of B.K. and the piano.

In an article in *Medical Problems of Performing Artists*, psychiatrist Peter F. Ostwald, relying on the ideas of D.W. Winnicott regarding transitional objects, supported the notion that the performer's relationship with the instrument and the interactive "loop established between the performer and the instrument" can be manifest as an internalized object "much as interactions with people can result in internalized representations of objects that come to life in dreams and fantasies. In this respect, music and musical instruments may have therapeutic functions in helping performers... to master loneliness, separation, and other painful emotional states" (Ostwald 1992, 111).

For violist E.M., the instrument symbolized his individuation struggles and his dysfunctional relationship with his father. Through improvisational directives, supported by therapist's techniques of mirroring, splitting, and pushing toward musical resolution, E.M. learned to express his inner relationship and fears regarding the viola. Where he had never brought himself to look closely at the instrument and enjoy its essence of wood, strings, and vibrations under his control, through our work, E.M. began to feel comfortable caressing the wood, tactically sensing the pressure of his finger on the strings and the pressure of his bow arm on the horsehair. He learned to look, feel, and embrace the viola as if he were symbolically embracing himself. He learned to improvise and play to enjoy himself, relishing the vibrations of the sounds in the wood and in his body. He achieved this through solo improvising of long, resonant tones, playing slowly to allow his inner mind-space to become filled with sound and vibrations.

For S.J., the violin symbolized her perfection and beauty. To her, the violin was a transitional object that helped her internalize her parents. It has become the symbol of their approval. She spoke of keeping the violin very close to her bed at night, even keeping it in its case at the foot of her blanket. In improvising with me the extremes of feelings and sounds she feared producing on the beautiful instrument and in verbally processing her feelings and insecurities about separation and individuation, S.J. could begin to understand issues involving this object. She was soon separating safely from her fears while she came closer to recognizing the violin as a reflection of herself and her musical essence. This was derived after many hours of work with free improvisation music therapy.

My role and interventions included much musical holding, reassurance, grounding, and mirroring her music to her. I also led her through many feelings, musical sounds, and rhythms that she seemed resistant to sense but that she was ultimately able to experience by following my leadership.

In working with the performer there seem to be problems warranting broader considerations than only those surrounding the singular performance event. Implicated are the level of performer comfort and confidence, not only with revealing and expressing one's emotional and psychological self in the music and feelings and attitudes toward the instrument, but also in *communicating* music and whatever it represents and embodies to the audience that expects this communication.

In the performance continuum, regardless of whether the music is improvised or composed, the issue of relatedness to one's instrument and one's revealed personal feelings, plus the need to resonate with what the composer reveals, addresses the musicianship portion of the piece beyond self-conscious, activity-related stress (See Figure 1, p. 13).

E.M., S.J., and B.K. were able not only to explore and discover new ways of expressing emotions, but because of my role as a safe, nonjudgmental listener/audience, each client learned to translate this sense of safety into a sense of self-confidence, thus reducing the fear of judgments. The music therapy process seems to have evolved an attitude not of judging, but of doing. It is exciting to realize that in working with performers, the music therapist has the distinct advantage of being able to address not only the psychological state of the performer, but the well-being of the *musical* state as well. In approaching the therapy work in this manner, the music therapist will encounter two or more discrete levels needing clinical scrutiny.

First is the client's identification and release of blocked emotions and conditioned attitudes which may be restricting a fully comfortable, confident, uninhibited infusion of oneself into the music and its ultimate projection outward to the audience. Second is the performance mind-set itself—what I call the battlefield attitude. These include the performer's preconditioned physical and mental reflexes and fears, relevant to the act of performance itself, that obstruct the performer's ability to experience a sense of security about technical and mental preparedness, expectations of a positive outcome, and the ability to be physically and mentally present and at ease in the flow of the music.

Blocks and mind-sets are typically approached as one single problem. In Montello's work, performance anxiety was approached as the main focus of the research, while resulting musicianship appeared as a by-product indicator of success.

I expanded on this by separating the two factors. Although a mutuality may exist between blocks and performance anxiety, there are times when blocks do not debilitate musicianship, when the music contains all the appropriate emotional content, but performance anxiety and panic in the battlefield due to improper mind-set is present. On the other hand, many confident, fully relaxed musicians who technically perform very well in the battlefield, communicate very little through the music. One cannot assume that emotional blocks and performance anxiety are always interrelated.

I address these two issues separately because in performance, regardless of what is about to be communicated, the performer must ultimately attain that "allowingness" state of transcendent mind that temporarily diminishes analytical-judgmental processes while the performer travels in the music. This means the performer *transcends* into a state of consciousness in which the music fully occupies the inner mind-space, temporarily receding left-brain analysis and judgment, allowing right-brain emotions and intuition to guide the flow of the music. This is the Zen moment when the music and musician become one.

E.M. achieved this state during one of our two-hour sessions. My directive was that he develop an improvisation using no more than four notes to be repeated as often, and in any variations, he desired. I served as the audience. "See if you can let me read your musical train of thought... try to engage my full attention to hearing in *my* head what you are hearing in yours as you play," I directed.

E.M. began on a long, low open C string, moving to F-F#-rest-rest-B. All notes were played on two lower strings. His patterns of rhythms repeated often, and his use of the four notes included interesting variations of bowings: long, short, staccato, fast, slow, loud, soft, and two at a time. He seemed to be having fun and appeared to be fully concentrating on the four tones. When he ended after approximately ten minutes, he said he had "lost track of time" and had become consumed by the possibilities that these four notes presented to his creative mind. He had not thought about me or whether he liked or disliked what he heard. Neither had he sensed any doubt that what he was doing was good. It never crossed his mind.

After our discussion about the four notes, I asked E.M. to choose one measure of any piece of repertoire and play that measure over and over, in any variations he desired, as he had just done with the four-note improvisation. He chose one measure of a Bach unaccompanied *Partita*. It involved nine notes in a specified rhythm which he was to obey. His freedom would be in bowing, dynamics, tempo, and tone quality, but he was to stay true to the written notation. He did this, repeating the measure as if on a tape loop for a few minutes, and then concluded. What happened? He had begun to think about Bach's style, bowing technique, posture, tone, what I might be thinking. Left brain had taken over.

I asked E.M. what the differences were between my directive involving only four notes and Bach's directive involving nine notes? "Oh... I don't know... do I have the same freedom just to be myself in Bach?" he asked. We discussed that in all instances E.M. was in charge. Nothing was different, except the preset notes and rhythms that Bach recommended. The objective was the same: to play with right-brain intuition, thinking only of the sound thoughts and how they entwine and evolve to produce a new universe of music.

E.M. and I devoted many subsequent sessions to this transcendence aspect of making music where music and musician become one.

Further in this chapter, in the section which discusses right brain and left brain, the reader will see it may be possible to condition the brain to allow the performer reflexive access to right-brain instinct, intuition, and feeling states while the left-brain analytic function can, for the most part, stay out of the picture.

CURING THE MUSIC, HEALING THE PERFORMER

In my work with E.M., S.J., and B.K. I observed that music therapy, approached from the musicianship point of view, helped in some ways to reduce or perhaps even bypass resistance to change. One possible reason for this could be music's natural impulse to move toward resolve (Stravinsky 1942), thus leaving less time for resistance to resolution and change.

When E.M., S.J., and B.K. created improvised music that they were unable to bring to resolution, they expressed a sense of frustration and incompleteness. My suggestions that they investigate elements which might have prevented resolution often met with a willingness to search more deeply into the emotions expressed during the improvisation and the particular here-and-now psychological processes at work, in order to discover possible musical resolutions. In some cases I joined in their endeavors while I was playing the piano by expanding and enhancing their music to help drive them beyond resistance toward a conclusion.

E.M., for instance, wanted to abandon a feeling of anger and frustration shortly after delving into an improvisation. Noticing his interest in evacuating, I began playing an energetic reflection of, and support for, his musical motifs and energies. When he abruptly stopped playing, I continued. After a few seconds, E.M. reconnected with his musical train of thought by playing energetically, becoming angrier and angrier, and finally shouting, "Stop! I'm exhausted!"

When we talked about his feelings, he said he felt pushed to continue when he wanted to quit and was becoming even angrier that I would not allow the music to stop. Quitting or absenting himself, rather than working through a feeling, is an issue for E.M. By my musical insistence that he continue, he had to work through his fear of feeling such intense anger, in order to reach the recognition point that instigated his cry to stop. I asked why he had not just stopped earlier. He responded that he knew that in spite of himself, he needed to continue, as I musically suggested, so as not to drop out as he is given to doing in his life. Further improvisational explorations aimed at resolving the music brought to resolution both musical and emotional issues presented. The anger at my not allowing him to stop translated into a wide variety of angers at other things in his life.

Another reason for lessened resistance could be the absence of suggestions relevant to abolishing old, long-standing emotional habits and personal connections. My ontological approach with clients was to stay in the present and encounter where and who they were at this time; what their current relationships were with their instruments, the music, the therapist, and their circumstances, as well as the general issues at hand.

S.J.'s Far Eastern upbringing included a great reverence for parental opinions that often caused her to suppress her true opinions and feelings in order to avoid being contrary. As was discussed earlier, at first S.J. was extremely resistant to opening up and flowing with her feeling impulses. She could not recognize them. She could not sense how these would feel. She felt that being less than beautiful, musically, and less than perfect meant being disloyal to her family and mentors.

Was S.J. hiding herself behind her music? She ultimately discovered that music was her screen from herself. As she began to open herself up to the various improvisation tasks I directed her to undertake, she began to see her inner self—the S.J. forbidden by cultural mores to emerge. There were no more excuses. She had a right to her opinions, angers, passions, and individuality. These were imperative requirements for honest musical expression.

I did not pressure her or the others for the alteration of past feelings and attitudes, but rather, for discovering feelings in the present, sensing them, becoming comfortable with them physically, psychologically, and musically, and eventually absorbing these first into the improvised music, then into the composed score. There was no implication to relinquish old allegiances or patterns. It was the client's option to retain or discard past attitudes and emotions; they were not applicable to the work at hand, which was the removal of emotional blocks in order to present genuine feelings freely and securely in the music.

In order to achieve this, however, the performer must ultimately revise certain constructs, even if only temporarily. In some cases, those momentary experiences precipitated longer lasting personal changes on the continuum of potential.

What actually transpired with E.M., as with S.J. and B.K., was that in identifying and musically expressing emotions that at one time may have been culturally or socially tabooed or repressed, the client became less blocked, less fearful of expression, and more comfortable with expression through both the improvised and the composed music. These new emotional freedoms were now becoming comfortable to live with, as they displaced old rigidities and repressions.

For instance, after a long weekend at home, usually the cause of much anxiety and anguish for E.M. (a male socialized to withhold tears and tantrums), I expected a regression to old blockages and a withholding of expression. Instead, E.M. reported that those old feelings were gone and he did not experience any of the usual emotional anxieties while he was at home. He seemed convinced that in learning to identify and express certain feelings, he experienced a catharsis that left him able to explore and discover new and different ways of expressing his emotional needs, which he did at home—to the surprise of his family and friends. "Somehow," he said, "what I'm learning in this therapy seems to cancel out ways I used to feel and act."

A similar occurrence happened to B.K., who was able to express his feelings safely to his father; and to S.J., who began to individuate emotionally and culturally from her traditionally inhibiting upbringing.

This was an interesting discovery. As the improvisations became more open and expressive, each client became more talkative and comfortable with himself or herself. When I asked each to parallel his or her improvised feeling into the scored music, there was a natural transition and consistency in the emotional ease and presence displayed within the composed music. Their playing changed. Their music changed. They changed.

I now asked: In treating performance problems, could the therapist aim to cure the music first, so to speak, and allow it to heal the performer, instead of the other way around? And, would this be as credible an approach as psychology-based music therapy, which seeks to heal the person first, resulting in better music only as a by-product?

In my work with E.M., S.J., and B.K., I had not set out to resolve the reasons for their blocks, but to identify that they existed. Rather than focusing on clients' reasons for closing off emotionally by asking for a recollection of past experiences, which in any case could be a distortion of actuality (Bergson 1959), I chose to help them identify their problems ontologically, thus leaving their adaptive options open. Do past reasons apply in the present? I often think perhaps not.

I was employing music therapy not so much to resolve psychological problems of the performer, but rather to resolve *musical* problems that created and/or amplified psychological stress and distress.

By my guiding the clients musically and verbally toward identifying the nature of their blocks and fears, and the impact of those upon the process of making music in the present, the clients were able to lessen resistance to self-disclosure, yield to a willingness to readapt, and move toward more immediate change. In short, we began to resolve the *now* that impacted the *then*, that in many instances, made the latter no longer applicable.

As in music, so in life. Freely improvised music allows emotional extremes to be explored within an accepting environment and become rechanneled into the music and into life, with slight stylistic temperance in deference to innate personality traits. This helps reestablish a sense of creative self-control without blocking emotions from either the music or the world at large. With further musical and psychological depth work, many readaptive components could become permanent positive enhancements in a client's personal interactive development with his or her world and his or her reality.

As music therapists, we devote much thought to identifying and justifying music as the healing agent. It seems logical that the focus on deriving healthy music could influence and infiltrate the healing process of the person who, after all, ends up being the one to perform this healthy music in the first place.

For the high-functioning but possibly neurotic performer, I discovered that by setting out to *cure the music*, that is, to address the issue of authentic emotional expression in repertoire, it is possible to simultaneously heal the inner being of the performer. In this case, the healing is the by-product of the music. What I arrived at is not a therapeutic coaching session. It is therapy's use of the free improvisation music-making process in response to particular musical, and therefore personal, issues and problems. It is coupled with an eclectic assemblage of verbal therapy theories and techniques to empower high-functioning cognition of, and connections between, the mind-body-spirit of the performer and the music he or she is performing. This provides a dynamic means of animating, within the music, the "allowingness" of knowing and doing.

Some of the psychological theories I relied on included existential/humanistic being there with the client in an allowing, accepting manner (Rogers 1961; May 1953, 1975, 1983; Maslow 1968, 1971; Yalom 1989); the object-relations and playing and reality theories of D.W. Winnicott (1991); the aspects of narcissism investigated by Alexander Lowen (1985); and the cognitive approaches as discussed and analyzed by Aaron Beck (1976), David Hargreaves (1986), and John Sloboda (1988).

I explored literature on the cognitive processes of improvisation and creativity, including studies on music cognition and improvisation undertaken by Jeff Pressing (1984,1988). He studied the role of improvisation in different artistic traditions and proposed several cognitive models for studying parallel conscious and unconscious processes in improvisation. I also relied on my own instinct and amalgam of knowledge compiled over my many years of study and professional experience.

LEFT BRAIN, RIGHT BRAIN

There is abundant physiologic evidence accumulating lately that seems to confirm the theory that the human brain processes information in two distinct ways: "(i) the rational, logical, time and language-based symbolic mode (which may possibly be 'left-brain-centered'); and, (ii) the intuitive, imaginative, perceptive, nontemporal, spatially-based creative mode (which may possibly be 'right-brain-centered')" (Schneck 1990, 70). "In other words," Dr. Schneck continues, "one might define two levels of consciousness in information processing, i.e., a cognitive level that functions primarily on verbal and other forms of sequential symbolism as a means for communication; and an instinctive, expressive level [not language-oriented] that functions primarily on a perceptual or sensual means for communication" (ibid.).

In the very complicated physiological process of metabolism involving the production of conjugate pairs of biochemical constituents, that is, enzymes, in response to internal and external stimuli to the brain, there exists the phenomenon of either producing or inhibiting production of one or the other of the conjugate pairs that carry relevant physiologic-function response messages throughout the body. Theoretically, when right-brain stimulation occurs, especially also involving the subcortical system that resonates with emotion and feeling sensations, if the right brain is busy, the production of specific reactive biochemical constituents will inhibit (regress) left-brain response activity and vice versa. This process, known as reciprocal inhibition, goes hand in hand in the performer with another physiologic function, that of *adaptation* (ibid., 458–59).

> Briefly described, adaptation occurs when: sensory inputs to the physiologic system develop response thresholds that depend on how persistent the [stimulus] is, such that if it becomes constant, the system essentially "ignores" it, and a greater stimulus is required to elicit a response.... On the other hand, facilitation and adaptation in many instances may gradually develop into conditioned reflexes, and may even reach the point wherein no sensory input is required anymore to elicit a particular response.

Thus, the first instance is one of recession, where a persistent stimulus, such as constant admonition for emotional expression, will eventually cause a recessive condition. In this case the brain ignores the persistent stimuli (i.e., both the admonitions and the emotions will eventually become regressed), ultimately reaching a state of indifference, emotionally and mentally.

The second instance is one of automatic recall, when a performer who drills his or her technique (left brain) for hours a day over the lifetime of basic training will go on automatic (remote) control, the conditioned reflex response, in technically reproducing the activity. In both instances, adaptive responses have become programmed into the computer, and the dance between recession and recall as well as right-brain or left-brain activity goes on.

As I view it, at least two components of Figure 1 (p. 13) can endure a state of recession, ignoring in the adaptive process, the potentially admonitory audience, including teachers, parents, competitors, composers, et al.

Automatic recall incorporates previous skills preparation. By performance time these have been well programmed into reflexive muscular and mental memorized responses to making music.

Relying on what I believe about the right and left brain and adaptive processes, I focused free improvisation activities not only toward instigating the discovery and unblocking of preset emotional conditions, but also toward helping reprogram these detrimental, maladaptive, emotional processes into healthier ones, and included newly found processes in an effort to widen adaptive choices.

Let us take the example of programming a newly discovered feeling that E.M. needed to encounter. E.M. and I spent many sessions attempting to elicit the feeling of extreme passion within him—love, anger, longing, desire—into his improvisations. It was not only a difficult emotion for E.M. to encounter but one for which E.M. thought he had no reference but, which Brahms required in the *Viola Sonata*. It was an arduous search for him. As a twenty-three-year-old male, he had by now been socialized by his background to contain himself "in an appropriate manner emotionally." He was fearful of discovering the feelings of inner passion and even more fearful of expressing them outwardly to others.

After several sessions of temporary resistance to full exploration, I decided to accompany him on the piano as a way of providing a role-model for musical expressions of passion as I sense it. He began solo, tentatively, and in slow, groping tones. I entered, atonally, and we began to interact in musical syntax and ride the sounds together. His playing soon took an independent direction by becoming very coarse and increasingly intense; he began repeating lower-register double-stops with a great sense of urgency, as if he were trying to saw the viola in half. His dynamic levels escalated and became increasingly harsh. At one point E.M. resembled Paganini flailing split bow hairs everywhere.

There was a great exigency about his playing. After I reflected and supported his intensity on the piano, encouraging him to continue and explore further, I began to play long holding clusters in twenty to thirty second intervals, over which he continued his fervent discourse. His resolution took on the resonance of the piano's open tenths chords and tone clusters. He chose to play within the middle register between the extreme ends of the piano sounds which I was resonating. The music resolved in a kind of major key tonality, and he ended on a long, open D string, on which he pondered for several seconds.

The improvisation lasted approximately fifteen minutes—quite a long time for such an intense explosion of energy! E.M. was exhausted... exhilarated... surprised, shocked... shaking... excited. He collapsed into the chair and allowed the silence to dissipate the still whirling illusions of sounds. I sat silently. When he finally spoke, he said he felt naked, weird, but as if he had experienced some sort of catharsis. He explained that he had never felt the sensations he felt during this experience: "in the gut of my being," as he described it, "there was this unraveling knot, and the more it unraveled, the larger and thicker it became." He explained a little about why he had never been allowed to express desire and passion. He liked having the knot "finally unravel."

He wanted to improvise again. This time I did not accompany him. Now that he had found the feelings within himself I did not want to influence his music in any way. His next improvisation, although somewhat less passionate, was as intense. But this time, it employed lengthier tones (rhythmically) and shortened sequences of syntax; it was less repetitive and often alternated between soothing and irritating dynamics. I felt as if he were really exploring all that he could find on the viola, relevant to feelings of passion. We both felt as if some kind of hurdle had been jumped.

In E.M.'s following session, although his mood was one of lethargy and depression, he said he wanted to return to the passion which he had often experienced during the week in the form of anger and irritability. His solo improvisation recalled all the qualities expressed in the previous session and was expanded by more secure bowing rhythms and technical displays. When I asked E.M. what he thought about and how he felt during this improvisation, he explained that he thought of all the ways Brahms expressed passion in the *Sonata*, but which E.M.'s viola instructor had been unable to evoke from him; and he felt very comfortable not only recalling the passion quality but outwardly expressing it. (He had passionately expressed his disapproval in an incident at his quartet rehearsal that week. It had been the first time he "ever had the guts to say anything.") I was delighted for E.M., and even more delighted for Brahms and the audience that would be listening to the *Sonata!*

This approach to adaptation and programming, rather than being purely behavioral/intellectual, is similar to approaches used in acting and movement improvisation (Spolin 1963) to reach, experientially, inner impulses and sensations that energize emotional expression. Continued improvisation sessions with E.M. brought about a kind of authentic emotional recall, some based on emotions which he experienced for the first time during our sessions. He developed new ways of being self-affirming and projecting his emotions throughout his music in a less self-conscious manner.

After working together only seven months, E.M.'s recital preparation took on a very positive forward thrust. He seemed more able to adapt his technical skills in the service of emotional (musical) expression that seemed to emanate confidently from within the contexts of his prepared music. Of special interest was his newly acquired understanding of himself and his own boundaries vis-à-vis the composer. He commented, "At last, I can really understand what it must have felt like for Brahms to want Clara Schumann, and even though I might express passion differently, I can still represent this feeling as if Brahms were doing it himself... and that makes me feel great!"

What resulted from E.M.'s improvisational work was the surfacing of his own unconscious feelings into the level of consciousness, enabling him to recognize and insert them, albeit in modified form, into the music of Brahms. My next goal was to help him quiet his performance anxieties related to technical control so that these would become preconscious (instinctive), in order to balance the conscious and preconscious in the creative act of performance.

Chapter 5

Toward the Zen of Performance

The right frame of mind for the artist is only reached when the preparing and the creating, the technical and the artistic, the material and the spiritual, the project and object, flow together without a break.

—Eugene Herrigel
Zen in the Art of Archery

LEARNING TO FOCUS, LEARNING TO HEAR

"How do I get my left brain to be quiet while my right brain does the work?" E.M.

One of the problems related to performance anxiety is the inability to trust the preconscious, fully focus on the music as evolving sound, and really hear the music as it is being played. "Consciousness is that which makes all things and events knowable.... When attention is allowed to rest in one place, it comes to know that place because attention is focused consciousness, and consciousness is that power of knowing" (Gallwey 1974, 114–115).

A well-known 20th-century composer once remarked that it does not matter whether all the notes are played correctly, since the audience does not hear all the notes, anyway. In fact, probably the only person who hears *all* the notes is the person playing them! For the performer the present is most often abandoned by worries about whether all the notes will be correctly played, glitches that just may have happened, concerns about problems recalled from the practice room, or those which may loom in the near future (Balk 1991, Caldwell 1990, Sarnoff 1987). Attempts at mental conditioning to quiet these worries and help relax the performer into the here-and-now are often addressed by verbal dictums: *Try to concentrate... tell yourself not to worry... do/ do not over-practice... tell the critics to fly a kite...* and so on. The problem is, if one is busy telling oneself to concentrate, one is not concentrating! And if one must incessantly talk oneself into calmness while performing, how can one focus on the music?

A healthy mind-set is one which is present all the time, not just onstage. Therefore, working toward attaining a stilled mind in order to live fully in the moment of music—especially for the performer who often repeats the act—can achieve a revised way of thinking in daily life. In this area especially, I have found that through improvisation therapy, the development of mental quieting and focus, and focused hearing, has helped establish an inner sense of peace and balance of mind-body-spirit—a Zen balance resulting in a sense of self-confidence and excitement about performance and about life. The act of expressing music can become as comfortable and unselfconscious for the performer as that of expressing a verbal thought. We never seem to worry about the misuse of language.

Music improvisation therapy is a way for the client to practice focusing on inner feelings in order to resonate with self needs and creative musical needs. A focused and quiet mind-set is imperative for fully hearing the inner being and the music. Learning to hear means to focus on listening in order to connect fully. According to Schneck, "the ears are... intimately connected with our perception of each other" (Schneck 1990, 56). "Through language and the making of sounds... [hearing is] also involved in our perception of the dimensions of time, especially as it relates to the inherent rhythm of music" (ibid., 55). We know drums were the earliest primitive instruments.

Scientists have postulated that pulsed sound stimuli somehow create a resonance with the natural clocks of the brain that ultimately control cyclic physiologic function, such as heartbeat and respiration rate, and behavior: "It is quite possible that many of the therapeutic effects of music... may be traced to the effect of rhythm on the subcortical structures of the brain as they relate to the perception of time and to the concept of pleasing resonance" (Schneck 1990, 56).

For the performer concentrating means focused hearing. This is the hearing that is simultaneous with the *doing*, not the thinking about it. The act of focused hearing applies to every phase of one's life, not just performance, as described above. How one focuses hearing can impact on human relations as well as music.

In preparing for his recital, E.M.'s ultimate fantasy was to present himself onstage with the full sense of confidence and knowingness that his emulated competitor always displays. When I first began to improvise with E.M. he was rigid, repetitive, self-conscious, worried, not very explorative, and often falling into prescribed technical syntax: scales, arpeggios, key-centered chords, long predictable bows, etc. He had never improvised before.

We played together. I followed his fluid, lyrical and atonal music by enhancing it with piano arpeggios and the full range of the instrument for some six minutes during our first session. When we finished, he stared at me with a look of complete surprise and said, "I never did anything like that before... oh, wow! That felt... weird." I asked him to describe what he had heard during the music: What had the piano played? What strings was he predominantly focused on? He had difficulty remembering... there was silence... and a look of sudden panic on his face: "Oh my God! I don't think I was even listening to the music!"

"What were you doing?" I asked. He proceeded to recite a standard list of left-brain functions: "I was wondering what you thought about what I was doing... I was trying to test the scales and arpeggios I missed in my lesson today... I was thinking about my lesson tomorrow... I felt very uncomfortable."

"About what?" I queried. "Hmm... about not knowing what to do!" There it was! Not only had he not heard himself play, he had never allowed himself simply to enjoy the freedom of exploring musical syntax without judgment or written directions. He was uncomfortable playing, performing, and being without restrictions.

One of the by-products of emotional blocks, and theoretically, a part of the narcissistic personality (Lowen 1985), is a strong dependency need. For E.M. this was defined in his obsessive need to practice a minimum of ten hours a day, and to rely heavily on teacher input and validation. This is common to musicians in general, but with E.M., teacher dependency seemed even more pronounced, and according to him, it was a pattern dating to his earliest days as a youngster. These needs included dependency on others for organization and information, on family for financial stability, on external opinions regarding mode of dress, types of activities, and travel. Dependency issues permeated E.M.'s life.

Making music requires independence and interdependence. Without detailing the psychological roots of E.M.'s problems, I can say that his dependency need created fear and anxiety about being onstage—the ultimate moment of independence for the musician. During E.M.'s obsessive hours of practice, he checked in often, i.e., he judged himself constantly during repertoire preparation, assessing to the extreme how he was doing technically. This judgment process repeated itself during his lessons at the conservatory, that were often invalidation sessions. His preoccupation with technical prowess took all his concentration and focus away from the fun and fulfillment of making music. Still, his compulsive practice habits did not better him technically. Technique was not his problem. This issue is pervasive among young performers today.

Five months following that first encounter, E.M. was much more explorative and musically independent, exhibiting confidence about his creative/ex-
pressive communication and his ability to express more fluently and authentically
in his own music and in written music. Our next step was to explore his capac-
ity to trust and fully depend on himself, to focus, hear, and ultimately transcend
anxiety and judgment in the battlefield of performance.

I returned to the physiologic concept of reciprocal inhibition (Chapter 4).
This can enable the right brain to continue the momentum of uninhibited self-
expression in the flow of the music, while left-brain analyses and judgments are
in abeyance.

By continued application of improvisation stimuli to right-brain intuition, could E.M.'s brain eventually adapt to a new habit of automatically re-
laxing left-brain judgement during the music-making activity? Could it relinquish his technique to the automatic pilot (preconscious) state, allowing him
to delve more fully into the inner streams of music imagery and thus enable
him to hear musical thoughts entwining and winding their way toward resolution, without left-brain interference?

It was time to explore this aspect of mental transcendence into a kind of
music meditation: the experience of flowing with the sounds as one would flow
in a stream of musical daydreams, without judgment or inhibition. It was time
to explore independence and a way for E.H. to relinquish himself to the music.

But what does it mean to relinquish oneself to the music? To flow with
the sound?

In helping E.M. prepare for the experience of this state of expanded consciousness and transcendence—in effect, helping him not to think, but to *do*—
I synchronized with the ideas stemming from a personal discussion with
Schneck about the constructs of continuum mechanics. In continuum mechanics a system is observed from an overall continuum precept, rather than
from close scrutiny of defined, detailed sequences of elements. Continuum
mechanics approaches an object as if there were no atomic or molecular structures within it, but instead exists as one continuous sequence—elements flowing and interacting with each other in one continuous motion—with no
discernible boundaries. The concept is akin to the idea of stepping back in order to see the whole.

This process is that which transforms the instrumentalist into the performer—the onstage ability to step back from the molecules and potentials for mishaps
in the microscopic elements, and to experience and be present in the whole music
as one single, continuous reality. It is another aspect of transcendence: the concept
of no discernible boundaries, no past or future, but only the present, where things
exist as a whole. By now the learned and rehearsed technical elements should have
internalized into preconsciousness or instinct. There should now exist a balanced

integration of right- and left-brain functions, enabling a higher level of consciousness—a transcendence into the meditative state in music.

I have had several performance experiences in which I transcended, at the end of which I surfaced as if from a dream. I helped E.M. explore these possibilities by instigating a type of toning activity on the viola (Keyes 1973).

The first time I introduced it, I asked E.M. to develop an improvisation on one open string of his choice. He was to play no other tones except that one open string. His task was to employ any bowing technique comfortable for him and produce any type of tone qualities and rhythms he wished. He could sit or stand—the only requirement was that he fully immerse himself into the listening and hearing of the tone: its spatial dimensions, intensities, qualities, resonances, characteristics, flaws, etc. He was to travel with it, if he could, as if the tone were a jet stream or river carrying him along. He was not to divert his focus from that tone but was to remain alert to any physical/mental imagery or sensations he felt.

By narrowing his margin of error to one item, he could concentrate his full attention on the tone. E.M. elected to sit while intoning the open C string, the viola's lowest string. He began by play very long, slowly drawn notes; his eyes were closed. I immediately observed a completely different, relaxed bowing arm. He was, without realizing it, employing the full length of the bow—something he rarely achieved when playing repertoire. After a few moments, his patterns became more rhythmic, some short, some long, some in quick succession; all were explorative of rhythmic variations. Soon, he also began pressing down on the bow, drawing coarser sounds, and alternately releasing the bow, drawing gentler ones. His improvisation went on for some eight to ten minutes, and it seemed as if he were fully mesmerized with the open C string. He seemed to reach a peak of energetic tonal thrusting and soon thereafter entered a state of musical resolution. He resolved in a slow fadeaway. E.M.'s spirit had transcended to a musical peak experience. When he ended his playing, he sat quietly with his eyes shut.

"Wow... what a great sound C is," he remarked, with his eyes still closed. "I feel dizzy." He said he felt every vibration of the sounds as if his entire body were creating them. He had a tactile sensation of being able to touch the sound's texture and thickness, and he felt his body flying and flowing with the sound stream. He had felt hot, cold, angry, loving, curious, careless, funny, sad, and happy. His eyes had welled with tears. His toes had "buzzed." He was not aware of his arms—not even the bowing arm—and seemed surprised when I shared my observations about his bowing. His overall sense was one of not being physically real—of not being a solid object—but rather of having become the tone. He had lost all track of time and place, and when he opened his eyes, he had forgotten where he was and that I was there. We repeated this experience in different ways for several weeks, and began to interject fragments of repertoire between similar viola tonings. E.M. was finally beginning to *hear* not only his music but himself in the world around him. His mind was learning to be stilled. His approach to external problems was becoming paced.

E.M.'s experiences help define my concept of musical transcendence. Something unusual took place for E.M. as a direct result of our improvisational work. He said he now realized that he had never *really* heard himself before. He sensed vibrations.

In recent sessions, he has retained the concept of hearing rather than thinking—of letting the music play him while he plays it. We are still uncovering and altering emotions, attitudes, moods, sensations, and psychological issues. E.M. faced graduate school auditions and a senior recital at the conservatory with a new sense of confidence. Since he began focusing attention on hearing his repertoire, our work seems to have lessened his anxiety considerably.

His musicianship has very obviously expanded, and his music is flowing more readily. He is much more present and secure, and has become much less dependent on his teacher, who according to E.M, has been detecting changes in E.M.'s playing. In fact, his ability to listen and hear have so expanded that he has become able to trust his own musical intuition, and in the process has become more self-dependent in many personal aspects of his life. He is self-confident in willing to risk being less than perfect. He has been accepted into the graduate programs of several prominent conservatories.

FREE IMPROVISATION THERAPY AND ZEN

In referring to the asset of creative intuition on the part of the music therapist, Mary Priestley touches upon a concept that is not only applicable to the therapist/client relationship but equally to the performer/music relationship. She states, "in the heat of the musical work he must feel and be and do. It is a kind of Zen in the art of musical relationship. Thinking is a crippling brake at such a time" (Priestley 1975, 198).

In *Zen in the Art of Archery,* Eugene Herrigel describes the Zen Master's theory of archery by citing the Master as follows:

> You must hold the drawn bowstring like a little child holding the proffered finger. It grips it so firmly that one marvels at the strength of the tiny fist. And when it lets the finger go, there is not the slightest jerk. Do you know why? Because a child doesn't think: *I will now let go of the finger in order to grasp this other thing....* Completely unselfconsciously, without purpose, it turns from one to the other, and we would say that it was playing with the things, were it not equally true that the things were playing with the child (Herrigel 1953, 30).

What resonates for me in both quotations above are: (a) the feeling, being, and doing in relation to the client, and in the performer's relationship to the music that parallels that of therapist/client; (b) *thinking* as a crippling brake in the process of being; (c) the idea of performing "completely unselfconsciously, without purpose," that is, allowing creativity to happen, unplanned, in the moment; and finally, (d) the idea that for the child who played with things, it was "equally true that the things were playing with the child."

Performance is not an analytical/cognitive process but an intuitive/creative one. All analyses and cognitive learning should have taken place in the practice room and become preconscious by now.

In performance, the Zen unity of mind-body-spirit finds a balance between right brain and left brain, so that transcendence into expanded states of consciousness can result, thus enabling an allowingness of the complete release of depth, letting the knowingness come through into the flow of the music and outward into the universe. This is the completely unselfconscious act of *allowing the music to play the performer.*

I use the term "expanded" rather than "altered" state of consciousness, because the performer is still fully present and consciously communicating with the audience. It is literally a state of mind of expanded awareness; a state in which left-brain cognitive function is in temporary recess while the right brain busily creates. Judgment is transcended, as is awareness of time, place, and self. *Performance* is a ceremony created under the inspiration of the moment.

> It does not depend on the bow, but on the presence of mind, on the vitality and awareness with which you shoot. Instead of reeling off the ceremony like something learned by heart, it will then be as if you were creating it under the inspiration of the moment, so that dance and dancer are one and the same (ibid., 55).

The art of life is in the moment of living. The art of music is in the moment of being. The united body and being of the musician performs; performer and music become one. "*It* takes the place of ego" (ibid., 76), and becomes greater than ego. Through music improvisation therapy, we have discovered that moment of living and doing without fear. In the end, the state of *Zen* is the state of *music*; the state of *music* is the state of *life*... *the* cosmic moment when everything the being is, becomes *it.*

Conclusion

Whenever I attempt to describe and share what I understand [about music therapy], I am struck by the limitations of words to communicate the experience of music and the deepest essence of life.

—Barbara Hesser
Music Therapy

Music therapy is a crucial missing link in the musician's development from technical instrumentalist to creative performer, as demonstrated in this study. It is ultimately this therapy process that consciously connects music to the being, enabling the performer to become healed by the very process of music-making he or she undertakes.

For the performer in particular, whose creative impulses encompass a plethora of anxieties and stresses, the unblocking of repressed emotions is a precursor to expressive musical authenticity. In addition, the role of the performer in relation to the composer, the audience, and the totality of the performance ritual demands the replacement of unnecessary distress and frustration with a confident state of mind, guaranteeing full freedom and presence in the music.

Through free improvisation therapy the musician can safely and creatively explore his or her inner being, and new ways of feeling, communicating, focusing, hearing, and unblocking repressed emotions and anxieties.

The complicated problems of the high-functioning but distressed musician requires a music therapist whose role is activated by the ability to listen as a therapist and hear as a musician. Such a music therapist will possess a comprehensive background encompassing a broad knowledge of music literature. He or she will have technical and improvisational skills on one or more instruments and extensive performance experience that enables full understanding of, and empathy with, the predicaments of modern day performers. The music therapist must also have a thorough grounding in psychological and developmental theories. The music therapist, employing free improvisation as a therapeutic technique, can: (a) appropriately reflect to the client what is heard, emotionally, tonally, and implied verbally; (b) assist the client in identifying neuroses which are detrimental to musical and personal well-being; (c) be a role model of musical definitions of emotions and attitudes; (d) link musical discoveries to the personal process—conscious, preconscious, unconscious; (e) focus the client toward full concentration, hearing and change; (f) help recycle discoveries made during free improvisations back into the performance repertoire, the performance act, and life itself; (g) ultimately provide the safe audience factor.

Marshall McLuhan once stated in an interview that "the play interval is important in converting facts into wisdom." Music improvisation therapy serves as that play interval. It enables the performer to convert into creative musical wisdom his entire factual being—all that he or she is, including the sum total of his or her conditioning and developmental processes which, were it not for a "fortunate error" (Cooper 1967, 20), would reduce the performer to what is conventionally accepted. *Inspiration,* not convention, is the inherent creative wisdom of the performer, the fortunate error that led him or her to the encounter with music in the first place.

The performer's musical expression must be projected out if it is to be shared with an audience. "Expressive features of performance are useless unless they can be detected by listeners. Similarly, it is pointless to expend energy on achieving levels of performance accuracy (for instance, in timing or tuning) that cannot possibly be appreciated by listeners, because the performance resolution is much finer than the discriminatory powers of listeners" (Sloboda 1985, 85). This involves careful focus and mental acuity in allaying technical fears in favor of the broader purpose of performing: communication and artistic sharing.

The concepts of right-brain/left-brain conditioning or reciprocal inhibition that allow the release of depth to happen while judgment subsides; the ideas borrowed from continuum mechanics of stepping back to see the whole are addressed by free improvisation in music therapy. They are developed in programming and reprogramming positive adaptive patterns of responses to musical and personal issues.

There is a Zen proverb that says: *He who has a hundred miles to walk should reckon ninety as half the journey* (Herrigel 1953, 54). On the music therapy road leading the performer toward inner peace and full artistic fulfillment, those first ninety miles wind from repression and fear, through exploration, innovation, identification, alteration, concentration, and readaptation to reconciliation, in which reproach and judgments are quelled, and then replaced by positive esteem, self-confidence, independence, and full creative potential.

Now the performer is ready to begin the final, most gratifying half of the journey *toward the Zen of performance.*

The murmur of the breeze in the trees, the rippling of a brook, the song of a bird... these natural sounds suggest music to us, but are not yet themselves music... they are promises of music; it takes a human being to keep them: a human being who is sensitive to nature's many voices... who feels the need of putting them in order and who is gifted for that task with a very special aptitude. In his hands all that I have considered as not being music will become music.

—Igor Stravinsky,
Poetics of Music

References & Recommended Reading

Abramson, R.M. (1980). Dalcroze-based improvisation. *Music Educator's Journal, 66*(5), 62–68.

Alvin, J. (1965). *Music for the handicapped child.* Oxford: Oxford University Press.

Alvin, J. (1978). *Music therapy for the autistic child.* London: Oxford University Press.

Alvin, J. (1981). Regressional techniques in music therapy. *Music Therapy, 1*(1), 3–8.

Apel, W. (1968). *Harvard dictionary of music* (20th ed.). Cambridge, MA: Harvard University Press.

Austin, D.S. (1986). *The healing symbol: Sound, song, and psychotherapy.* Unpublished master's thesis. New York University, School of Education, Health, Nursing, and Arts Professions, New York.

Balk, H.W. (1991). *The radiant performer.* Minneapolis: University of Minnesota Press.

Beck, A.T. (1976). *Cognitive therapy and emotional disorder.* New York: Meridian/Penguin.

Bergson, H. (1959). *Matter and memory.* New York: Anchor Books.

Boxill, E.H. (1981). A continuum of awareness: Music therapy with developmentally handicapped. *Music Therapy, 1*(1), 17–23.

Boxill, E.H. (1985). *Music therapy for developmentally disabled.* Austin, TX: Pro-Ed.

Bruscia, K., Hesser, B., & Boxill, E. (1981). Essential competencies for the practice of music therapy. *Music Therapy, 1*(1), 43–49.

Caldwell, R. (1990). *The performer prepares.* Dallas, TX: Pst..., Inc.

Campbell, J., with Moyers, B. (1988), *The Power of Myth.* New York: Doubleday

Clark, D.B., & Agras, W.S. (1991, May). The assessment and treatment of performance anxiety in musicians. *American Journal of Psychiatry, 148*(5), 598–605.

Cooper, D. (1971). *Psychiatry and anti-psychiatry.* New York: Ballantine Books.

Copland, A. (1952). *Music and imagination.* New York: Mentor Books.

Davis, M., & Wallbridge, D. (1990). *Boundary and space: Introduction to the work of D.W. Winnicott.* New York: Bruner/Mazel.

Doerschuk, B. (1984, October). The literature of improvisation. *Keyboard, 10,* 48–52.

Gallwey, W.T. (1974). *The inner game of tennis.* New York: Bantam.

Gardner, H. (1983). *Frames of mind: The theory of multiple intelligences.* New York: Basic Books.

Green, B., & Gallwey, W.T. (1986). *The inner game of music.* New York: Anchor Press/Doubleday.

Hargreaves, D.J. (1986) *The developmental psychology of music.* Cambridge, MA: Cambridge University Press.

Havas, K. (1973). *Stage fright: Its causes and cures.* London: Bosworth.

Herrigel, E. (1953). *Zen in the art of archery.* New York: Pantheon Books.

Hesser, B. (1988). Statement. *Music Therapy, 7*(1), 70–71.

Keyes, L.E. (1973). *Toning: The creative power of the voice.* Marina del Rey, CA: DeVorss.

Kubie, L. (1961). *Neurotic distortion of the creative process.* New York: Noonday Press.

Lowen, A. (1985). *Narcissism: Denial of the true self.* New York: Collier Macmillian.

Maslow, A.H. (1968). *Toward a psychology of being.* New York: Van Nostrand Reinhold.

Maslow, A.H. (1970). *Religions, values and peak-experiences.* New York: Penguin Group.

Malsow, A.H. (1971). *The farther reaches of human nature.* New York: Penguin Group.

May, R. (1953). *Man's search for himself.* New York: Dell

May, R. (1975). *The courage to create.* New York: Bantam Books.

May, R. (1983). *The discovery of being. Writings in existential physhology.* New York: W.W. Norton

May, R. (1991). *The cry for myth.* New York: Delta Publications.

Montello, L. (1986). *Music therapy: A holistic paradigm for the treatment and prevention of stress in the professional musician.* Unpublished master's thesis, New York University School of Education, Health, Nursing and Arts Professions, New York: New York University.

Montello, L. (1989). *Utilizing music therapy as a mode of treatment for the performance stress of professional musicians.* Unpublished doctoral dissertation, New York University School of Education, Health, Nursing and Arts Professions, New York.

Nordoff, P. & Robbins, C. (1977). *Creative music therapy.* New York: John Day.

Ostwald, P.F. (1992). Psychodynamics of musicians: The relationship of performers to their musical instruments. *Medical Problems of Performing Artists, 7*(4), 110–113.

Pressing, J. (1984). Cognitive processes in improvisation. In W.R. Crozier & A.J. Chapman, (Eds.), *Cognitive perception of art* (pp. 345–363). Amsterdam: Elsevier.

Pressing, J. (1988). Improvisation: Methods and models. In J.A. Sloboda, (Ed.), *Generative processes in music* (pp. 129–178) Oxford: Clarendon Press.

Priestley, M. (1975). *Music therapy in action.* London: Constable Press.

Ristad, E. (1982). *A soprano on her head.* Moab, UT: Real People Press.

Rogers, C.R. (1961). *On becoming a person—a therapist's view of psychotherapy.* Boston: Houghton-Mifflin.

Sarnoff, G. (1987). *Never be nervous again.* New York: Crown Publishers.

Schneck, D.J. (1990). *Engineering principles of physiologic function.* New York: New York University Press.

Sessions, R. (1950). *The musical experience of composer, performer, listener.* Princeton, NJ: Princeton University Press.

Stephens, G. (1983). The use of improvisation for developing relatedness in the adult client. *Music Therapy, 3*(1), 29–42.

Sloboda, J. (1985). *The musical mind: The cognitive psychology of music.* Oxford: Clarendon Press.

Sloboda, J. (Ed.). (1988). *Generative processes in music: The psychology of performance, improvisation and composition.* Oxford: Clarendon Press.

Spolin, V. (1963). *Improvisation for the theater. a handbook of teaching and directing techniques.* Evanston, IL: Northwestern University Press.

Stravinsky, I. (1942). *Poetics of music.* Cambridge, MA: Harvard University Press.

Tyson, F. (1979). Child at the gate: Individual music therapy with a schizophrenic woman. *Art Psychotherapy, 6,* 77–83.

Tyson, F. (1981). *Psychiatric music therapy: Origins and development.* New York: Creative Arts Rehabilitation Center.

Winnicott, D.W. (1991). *Playing and reality.* London: Routledge.

Yalom, I.D. (1989). *Love's executioner and other tales of psychotherapy.* New York: Harper Perennial.